# Christian Communicators Conference

EXPLORE • EQUIP • EXPAND

2025

## Dear Sister,

Welcome to the Christian Communicators Conference!

Whether you traveled across the country or just down the road, know this—you belong here.

Maybe you arrived with a full heart and a clear calling. Or perhaps you're wondering if your voice matters, if your story is ready, or if you truly have a place here. Hear this: you are seen, you are called, and you are not alone.

This is more than a conference—it's a sacred space. A refueling station. A launchpad for the work God is preparing in you. You are surrounded by a sisterhood of faith-filled women boldly sharing the messages God has placed on their hearts. Your voice matters, and these four days are set apart for sharpening your skills, deepening your faith, and stepping into your calling with confidence.

So, here's your invitation:

> Be open—God may speak through a keynote, a breakout session, a practice round, or even a conversation over coffee.

> Be bold—Ask the question. Share the idea. Step into the opportunity that feels just out of reach.

> Be expectant—God is already moving. Lean in and receive what He has prepared for you.

Together, we'll learn, worship, and grow. And by the time we leave, our hope is that you'll not only feel more equipped but more assured in who you are and Whose you are.

You were led here on purpose. For a purpose.

And we are so grateful you said yes.

With joy and anticipation,

Pam Mitchael

Director, Christian Communicators Conference

# Schedule

## WEDNESDAY, JULY 23RD

| Time | Session/Activity | Location | Page |
|---|---|---|---|
| 1 PM | Registration Open | Ballroom Foyer | |
| 3 PM | Hotel Checkin Opens | | |
| 11-5 PM | Photo Sessions & Color Analysis (By Appointment) | TBD | |

### PRE-CONFERENCE SESSIONS

| Time | Session/Activity | Location | Page |
|---|---|---|---|
| 1:30-3 PM | Andrea Lende: Holy Spirit & High-Tech | Spring Creek | 13 |
| 3:15–4:45 PM | Linda Goldfarb: How to Add Pop & Pizazz in Your Presentation | Spring Creek | 15 |
| 6 – 7:30 PM | Complimentary Dinner Available (Provided by the Hotel) | Lobby Area | |

### CONFERENCE KICKS OFF

| Time | Session/Activity | Location | Page |
|---|---|---|---|
| 7-7:45 PM | Welcome | Renner | |
| 7:45-8 PM | Praise & Worship | Renner | |
| 8-8:45 PM | Keynote Speaker: Mary DeMuth | Renner | 17 |
| 8:45 PM | Closing | Renner | |

## THURSDAY, JULY 24TH

| Time | Session/Activity | Location | Page |
|---|---|---|---|
| 6:30-8 AM | Complimentary Breakfast Available (Provided by the Hotel) | Hotel Lobby | |
| 8 AM | Conference Room Opens Daily (Doors close at 8:30) | Renner | |

## THURSDAY, JULY 24TH

| Time | Session/Activity | Location | Page |
|---|---|---|---|
| 8:30-8:45 AM | Praise & Worship | Renner | |
| 8:45-9 AM | Morning Devotion – Yvette Walker | Renner | |
| 9-10:30 AM | Linda Goldfarb: Finding Your Niche | Renner | 21-23 |
| 10:30-10:45 AM | Break | Renner | |
| 10:45-12 PM | Mary R. Snyder: Open Strong | Renner | 25-27 |
| 12-1 PM | Lunch – Provided | Ballroom Foyer | |
| 1-2 PM | Linda Goldfarb: Refine Your Voice | Renner | 29-33 |
| 2-3:30 PM | Mary R. Snyder: Speak It In 60 | Renner | 35-37 |
| 3:30-3:45 PM | Break | | |
| 3:45-4 PM | Panel | Renner | |
| 4 PM | Mary Snyder: Intro Reel Workshop | Renner | 39 |
| 6:30 | Complimentary Dinner Available (Provided by the Hotel) | Hotel Lobby | |
| 7:30-8:30 PM | Optional Coaching Sessions | To Be Assigned | |

## Friday, JULY 25TH

| Time | Session/Activity | Location | Page |
|---|---|---|---|
| 6-8:30 AM | Complimentary Breakfast Available (Provided by the Hotel) | Renner | |
| 8 AM | Conference Room Opens (Doors close at 8:30) | Renner | |
| 8:30-8:45 AM | Praise & Worship | Renner | |
| 8:45-9 AM | Morning Devotion – Christine Hoy | Renner | |
| 9-10:30 AM | Mary Snyder: The Business Side of Speaking | Renner | 43-45 |

# Schedule

## Friday, JULY 25TH

| Time | Session/Activity | Location | Page |
|---|---|---|---|
| 10:30-10:45 AM | Break | Hotel Lobby | |
| 10:45-11:15 AM | Kim Kimble: What Event Planners Need | Renner | 47 |
| 11:15-12 PM | Andrea Lende: Self-Publishing Landscape | Renner | 49-51 |
| 12-2 PM | Lunch – On your own | | |
| 2-3:30 PM | Victoria Chapin: Let's Get Social | Renner | 53-55 |
| 3:30-3:45 PM | Break | | |
| 3:45-5:30 PM | Judy Bone: Style & Shine | Renner | 57-61 |
| 6:30 PM | Complimentary Dinner Available (Provided by the Hotel) | Lobby Area | |
| 7:30-8:30 PM | Practice Groups & Feedback | To Be Assigned | |

## Saturday, JULY 26TH

| Time | Session/Activity | Location | Page |
|---|---|---|---|
| 6-8:30 AM | Complimentary Breakfast Available (Provided by the Hotel) | Hotel Lobby | |
| 8 AM | Conference Room Opens Daily (Doors close at 8:30) | Renner | |
| 8:30-8:45 AM | Praise & Worship | Renner | |
| 8:45-9:15 AM | Morning Devotion – Kim Dotson | Renner | |
| 9:15 AM | Intro Reels – Filming Session | Renner | |
| 12:30 PM | Free time | | |
| | Photo & Color Analysis (by Appointment) | | |
| 7 PM | Red Carpet Night Dinner | Renner | |

## Sunday, JULY 27TH

| Time | Session/Activity | Location | Page |
|---|---|---|---|
| 6-8 AM | Complimentary Breakfast Available (Provided by the Hotel) | Hotel Lobby | |
| 8 AM | Conference Room Opens Daily (Doors close at 8:30) | Renner | |
| 8:30-8:45 AM | Praise & Worship | Renner | |
| 8:45-9:15 AM | Morning Devotion – Andrea Lende | Renner | |
| 9:15 AM – 10:30 AM | Closing Ceremony | Renner | |

# Welcome, Beautiful Communicator

Before we begin our time together, take a few quiet moments to reflect—not just on what you hope to gain, but on what your heart is longing for. Invite God into your time here.

What is stirring in your heart as you begin this journey?

What do you hope to discover or receive while you're here?

What do you need from God to move forward in your calling?

Complete this sentence: By Sunday, I hope to…

As you move through our time together, you'll find plenty of room throughout this book to reflect, jot down notes, and record the precious aha moments that speak to your heart. Be on the lookout for new insights and all the things you came here to receive. In Matthew 7:7 (NIV), Jesus said, "Ask and it will be given to you; seek and you will find; knock and the door will be opened to you." Let's ask, seek, and knock over these next few days together. God is sure to provide!

## Watch for:

Insights you can use immediately: simple tools often spark the greatest change.

Connections that matter: the women God places in your path.

Clarity on your next steps: what God is calling you toward.

As a precursor to this conference, we'd also like to suggest that you…

## Find Your Three:

One of the most valuable things you can do this weekend is identify your support network. During the conference, we invite you to prayerfully discover your three people—a mentor, an accountability partner, and a friend—who will walk alongside you in your calling. At the end of this guide, you'll find space to record the names of those who will become part of your support circle and your team for the journey ahead.

A Mentor: Who speaks into your calling? Whose voice do you trust?

An Accountability Partner: Who will help you when things get hard?

A Friend: Who can you laugh with, cry with, pray with? Who will cheer you on?

This is more than a conference. This is a launching pad. Let's begin…

# Wednesday

# Daily Reflection

Ephesians 2:10 (NIV)

*For we are God's handiwork, created in Christ Jesus to do good works, which God prepared in advance for us to do.*

You are God's masterpiece—uniquely created and intentionally placed in this moment for a **reason**. Long before you arrived at this conference, He prepared something **beautiful** for you to step into. We invite you to walk into the fullness of His plan for you. You were made for this.

What does it mean that God prepared good works in advance—just for you?

How do you feel called to serve or impact others?

# Christian Communicators Conference

## Aha Moments

## 3 Takeaways

1.

2.

3.

## Andrea Lende
## Holy Spirit & High-Tech

**Day 1**

# Christian Communicators Conference

## Aha Moments

## 3 Takeaways

1.

2.

3.

# Linda Goldfarb

## How to Add Pop & Pizazz to Your Presentation

*Day 1*

# Christian Communicators Conference

## Aha Moments

## 3 Takeaways

1.

2.

3.

# Mary DeMuth

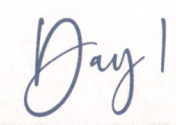

## The Courage to Communicate

# Thursday

## Daily Reflection

### Ephesians 3:20 (AMPC)

*Now to Him Who, by (in consequence of) the [action of His] power that is at work within us, is able to [carry out His purpose and] do super-abundantly, far over and above all that we [dare] ask or think [infinitely beyond our highest prayers, desires, thoughts, hopes, or dreams]*

God's power isn't just around you—it's alive and active within **you**.

He is able to do far more than you've dared to ask, imagine, or dream.

Know that even your quietest **hopes** and deepest desires are seen.

He's not only listening; He's already at work.

What are you dreaming about with God today?

Write down the hopes and desires that He's stirring in your heart, and invite Him to do more than you can imagine.

# Christian Communicators Conference

## Aha Moments

## 3 Takeaways

1.

2.

3.

*Linda Goldfarb*

Day 2

## Finding Your Niche

### Centering Your Talk Around God's Purpose

Identifying our niche is more than where we hope to be speaking; it's where God has designed us to speak.

### Some thoughts to consider:

- What comes naturally to you?
- Where do you feel most at ease?
- Where do you sense the presence of the Holy Spirit?
- Are you available to travel?
- What is the best setting for your subject matter?
- Can you teach material from other people?
- Can your talk be a series?

NOTES:_____

_____

### Option 1: Small Group Leader

- Local
- Pre-planned Material (yours or others)
- Social Environment
- Community Building

NOTES:_____

_____

## Option 2: Workshop Instructor

Local/Virtual/Conferences

Pre-planned Material

Social Environment

One-off Teaching

NOTES: _____

_____

## Option 3: Stage Presenter

Local or Traveling

Large Group Focus

Social Environment

Short or Long-term Engagements

NOTES: _____

_____

## Option 4: Professional Trainer/Coach

Accreditation and or Certifications

Group or Individual

Follow Up System

In-person or Virtual

NOTES: _____

_____

*Day 2*

## Option 5: Keynote Speaker

Local/Virtual/Conferences

Expertise – Book – References

Social Environment

Community Building Long Term

NOTES:_____

_____

## Final Thought from Linda:

Zechariah 4:10 (NLT)

*Do not despise these small beginnings, for the Lord rejoices to see the work begin…*

# Christian Communicators Conference

## Aha Moments

## 3 Takeaways

1.

2.

3.

*Mary R. Snyder*

*Day 2*

## Open Strong

## Workshop Worksheet: Captivate from the Start

## Crafting an Opening That Grabs Attention + Keeps It

### Why This Matters:

You've got **7 seconds** to catch your audience's attention. If you open weak, they're already checking out—scrolling their phone in their mind, if not their hands.

But if you open with a powerful story, question, or emotional punch… they'll lean in and stay with you. Let's craft that moment.

### Step 1: Reflect

Let's dig for gold in your own life.

Answer these prompts with quick honesty—no polishing yet:

1. A moment when everything changed for me:
   _____
   _____

2. A funny, embarrassing, or unexpected story I always find myself telling:
   _____
   _____

3. A moment of tension, failure, or breakthrough in my journey:
   _____
   _____

4. What does this story *reveal* about the heart of my message?
   _____
   _____

## Step 2: Pick Your Opening Strategy

## Choose one of the following "hooks" to develop:

**Start with story**

"Let me tell you about the day I almost quit speaking…"

"It was a Tuesday. I was late. And I had toilet paper stuck to my shoe…"

**Ask a bold question**

"Have you ever begged God to use you, but then your dodged every opportunity?"

"What if the thing you're afraid to say is exactly what they need to hear?"

**Drop them in the middle of the story**

"I was standing backstage, hands shaking, wondering why I said yes to this."

"There were 300 women in the room, and I can't remember what I want to say!"

*Day 2*

## Step 3: Draft Your Captivating Opening

Choose one story or moment from above and craft a 3–4 sentence opening. Keep it emotionally engaging and connected to your core message.

Write your draft here:

_____

_____

_____

_____

_____

## Final Tip from Mary:

*Your opening isn't the warm-up—it's the front door. Make it irresistible.*

Try it out loud. Adjust as needed. And most importantly? Use it.

_____

_____

_____

_____

# Christian Communicators Conference

## Aha Moments

## 3 Takeaways

1.

2.

3.

*Linda Goldfarb*
Refine Your Voice

## Making the Most of What God Gave You

**Vocal Care for Voice Professionals**

**Stay hydrated.**

Drink ½ body weight in ounces of room temperature water daily.

A hydrated body produces beautiful skin, hair, and energy.

**Use a warm steam humidifier.**

Daily use helps keep the sinuses clear.

**Relax your vocal cords.**

Blend a tablespoon of raw honey with hot herbal tea and fresh lemon.

Drink 30-45 minutes before you speak.

**Never clear your throat.**

Audible clearing damages your vocal cords.

Choose to swallow deeply. Repeat as needed.

Biting into a slice of green apple (such as Granny Smith) promotes saliva production and helps alleviate dry mouth.

**Refrain from dairy and caffeine products before you speak.**

Dairy causes mucus drainage.

Caffeine dehydrates vocal membranes.

**Rest your voice.**

> Daily moments of silence and solitude enhance our spiritual growth and vocal health.
>
> Consider 30 minutes a day as a starting point.

## Trusting Your "True" Professional Voice

Whether you are a Get-it-Done Mobilizer, Life-of-the-Party Socializer, Keep-the-Peace Stabilizer, Everything-in-Order Organizer, or a blend of two or three, you are designed exactly as God intends for you to be used to glorify Him.

**What's your personality type?**

> Mobilizer
>
> Socializer
>
> Stabilizer
>
> Organizer
>
> Blend of—

**What do you recognize about your personality in front of people?**

> Do you naturally smile when speaking?
>
> Do you move rhythmically or mechanically?
>
> Where do you focus when speaking?

**How do you feel about the tone, pace, and quality of your voice?**

> Do you talk fast, slow, or just right?
>
> Do you enunciate with clarity?
>
> Do you have a cultural dialect?

No matter your personality or verbal delivery, you can be a successful speaker.

*Day 2*

## Recognizing & Eliminating "Ticks" and Filler Words

### Become Aware

Record yourself – audio and video recordings work best.

Ask for feedback.

### Address Body Ticks

Identify physical habits.

Tend to fidget?

Use warm-up activities.

Use hand gestures strategically.

### Reduce Filler Words

Pause first – embrace the power of silence.

Speak slower.

Prepare, prepare, prepare.

Use simpler words.

Practice with bullet point prompts.

Be patient with yourself and focus on clarity and connection, rather than perfection.

NOTES:_____

_____

_____

## Know Your Microphone Options

### Podium

Not always the favorite, yet very usable.

### Handheld

With a cord or cordless.

A floor stand may be available.

Great for audience participation.

### Lapel

Clipped to your clothing.

Most require a body pack – consider your clothing.

Consider the location of the bodypack.

Directional mic – be aware of location for best amplification.

### Countryman

The best choice for those who enjoy using their hands and moving a lot.

A bodypack is also required.

Which would you choose? _____

NOTES: _____

_____

_____

_____

_____

Day 2

**Final Tip from Linda:**

*"Claim your voice as God's gift and use it wisely for His glory."*

# Christian Communicators Conference

## Aha Moments

## 3 Takeaways

1.

2.

3.

*Mary R. Snyder*

Day 2

"Speak It In 60"

# Crafting Your Elevator Pitch with Purpose + Power

## What's an Elevator Pitch—And Why Does It Matter?

This isn't about sounding impressive. This is about being **clear**, **compelling**, and **confident** when someone asks: "So, what do you speak about?"

A great pitch opens doors, starts conversations, and gives you the confidence to *own your calling*.

### Step 1: Brainstorm Before You Build

Let's dig in with some quick prompts. Don't overthink—just spill the good stuff:

**Who has God called you to speak to?**

(Be specific! Moms in ministry? Women in recovery? High-achieving perfectionists?)

_____

_____

**What transformation do you help them experience?**

(What shifts after they hear your message?)

_____

_____

**What makes your voice/message different?**

(Life experience, teaching style, biblical focus, sense of humor, etc.)

_____

_____

**Why does this message matter to you?**

_____

_____

## Step 2: Build the First Draft

Use this flexible framework to start crafting your pitch. Tweak the words to sound like you—this isn't a script, it's a starting point.

**"I help [audience] [transformation] by [how you deliver it]."**

Example: "I help women who feel stuck in self-doubt find freedom and clarity through biblical truth and storytelling."

Now you try: _____

_____

_____

_____

### Step 3: Say It Out Loud

Read it aloud. How does it feel in your mouth?

Imagine saying it to someone at a coffee shop. Does it invite conversation?

Ask a friend or tablemate: "Does this sound like me?"

**Final Draft (for now!):**

_____

_____

_____

### Final Tip from Mary:

*Clarity beats clever. Say it plain, say it strong, and let God do the rest.*

_____

_____

_____

_____

_____

_____

# Christian Communicators Conference

## Aha Moments

## 3 Takeaways

1.

2.

3.

# Mary R. Snyder

## Intro Reel Workshop

**Day 2**

# Friday

## Daily Reflection

Isaiah 40:31 (AMPC)

*But those who wait for the Lord [who expect, look for, and hope in Him] shall change and renew their strength and power; they shall lift their wings and mount up [close to God] as eagles [mount up to the sun]; they shall run and not be weary, they shall walk and not faint or become tired.*

You may feel tired and worn, but God has not forgotten you. He strengthens those who **wait** on Him. He knows you, your season, and your story. He'll meet you right where you are with fresh **strength**, **hope**, and a **future** that will unfold with purpose. It's not too late. In His hands, it never is.

Where do you need God's strength today?

What part of your story do you need Him to breathe new life into?

# Christian Communicators Conference

## Aha Moments

## 3 Takeaways

1.

2.

3.

*Mary R. Snyder*

**Day 3**

## The Business Side of Speaking

## Treat Your Calling Like the Business God's Called You to Build

### Why This Matters:

God gave you a message.

But here's the truth: you can't share that message if you're burnt out, broke, and overbooked doing free events with no boundaries.

It's time to build a *sustainable* speaking ministry—one that honors your calling, your time, and your purpose.

*By wisdom a house is built, and through understanding it is established.*
Proverbs 24:3

### The Foundations of Your Speaking Business

Use this as your starter checklist—mark what you already have and what you need to work on.

### Clarity of Message + Audience

☐ I can clearly state who I serve and what transformation I offer.

☐ My message is focused and tied to my personal story/testimony.

### Professional Assets

☐ Headshot

☐ Speaker bio (short + long)

☐ Speaker one-sheet

☐ Website or speaker page

☐ Speaker reel or 2–3 images of you speaking (until you have that speaker reel)

**Pricing Structure**

☐ I have my booking fee to speak

**Booking & Admin Systems**

☐ I have a simple booking process

☐ I use contracts and collect info from event hosts

☐ I track mileage, travel, expenses, etc.

**Marketing & Visibility**

☐ I show up online consistently

☐ I grow my email list

☐ I network with churches, ministries, and other speakers

☐ I follow up with past hosts

**Mindset Shifts I'm Making**

Fill in what speaks to you:

I will stop apologizing for _____

_____

*Day 3*

I'm ready to start treating my speaking as _____

_____

Stewardship means _____

_____

**Your Next Bold Step**

Check one (or add your own):

☐ Create my speaker one-sheet

☐ Raise my rates / or start charging to speak

☐ Reach out to 3 potential events

☐ Create a speaker info page

☐ Start tracking income & expenses

☐ Schedule time to work on my business

My next brave move: _____

## Final Tip from Mary:

*You're not charging for the Gospel. You're charging for the time, wisdom, and preparation it takes to deliver it with excellence.*

Own your role. You're the messenger and the manager of your calling.

# Christian Communicators Conference

## Aha Moments

## 3 Takeaways

1.

2.

3.

## Kim Kimble

## What Event Planners Need

**Day 3**

# Christian Communicators Conference

## Aha Moments

## 3 Takeaways

1.

2.

3.

*Andrea Lende*

Publishing

*Day 3*

## Navigating the Self-Publishing Landscape

### Traditional Publishing

**Pros**

Publishing company backing

Professional guidance

Publishing is likely

**Cons**

Typically requires a large platform

Length of time to publish

Lose autonomy

Publisher owns rights to your manuscript

### Hybrid Publishing

**Pros**

No platform needed

Semi-professional guidance

Publication is likely

**Cons**

High costs

Potential quality issues

Publisher's timeline

Loss of control

## Self-Publishing

**Pros**

No platform required

Full control

Shorter time to publish

Retain rights

Free to publish on Amazon and IngramSpark

Print-on-demand distribution

You determine the price of your book

**Cons**

Steep Learning Curve

# Self-Publishing Benefits

**You're the Boss of Your Book**

No gatekeepers. It's your story—your way.

**Publish on Your Timeline**

Upload and publish in days or weeks.

*Day 3*

**You Own It All**

Retain all rights to your manuscript.

Earn up to 70% royalties on eBooks.

Run your own sales and promotions.

## What Option Feels Right for You and Why?

Traditional: _____

_____

_____

Hybrid: _____

_____

_____

Self-Publishing: _____

_____

_____

Notes: _____

_____

_____

# Christian Communicators Conference

## Aha Moments

## 3 Takeaways

1.

2.

3.

# Victoria Chapin

## Let's Get Social

## Marketing God's Way

**Yield to the Holy Spirit; be the light and the voice of truth!**

Hebrews 13:16 (ESV)

*Do not neglect to do good and to share what you have, for such sacrifices are pleasing to God.*

**Identify:**

Your Why _____

_____


Your Who _____

_____


Your Where _____

_____


Your What _____

_____


Your When _____

_____

Day 3

## Four Kinds of Followers:

1. _____
2. _____
3. _____
4. _____

## How-Tos and Hands-On for Facebook and Instagram:

Posts/Carousels _____

Reels _____

Stories _____

Live Videos _____

## Do's and Donts:

Do:

_____

_____

_____

_____

*Day 3*

Don't:

_____
_____
_____
_____

## What's Working Now?

_____
_____
_____
_____
_____
_____
_____
_____

# Christian Communicators Conference

## Aha Moments

## 3 Takeaways

1.

2.

3.

*Judy Bone*

Style & Shine

Day 3

## Let the Inside Shine Bright on the Outside

Psalm 139:14 (NIV)

*I praise you because I am fearfully and wonderfully made;
your works are wonderful; I know that full well.*

You are a beautiful creation of God—no matter your size, age, or shape! Let's learn to reflect the beauty within through style choices that honor God and highlight your best features.

### Color Me Confident: Finding Your Best Hues

Universal Colors That Flatter Everyone: Burgundy, Periwinkle, Navy, Red, Turquoise

**Your Personalized Color Code (Hair, Skin, Eyes, and Contrast Level):**

C _____ – Dark Hair, Fair/Medium Skin, Bright Eyes

C _____ – Ash-Toned Hair (Silver, White, Gray), Mixed Skin/Eye Tones

D _____ – Dark Hair, Medium-Deep Skin, Dark Eyes

L _____ – Blonde or White Hair, Fair Skin, Light Eyes

S _____ – Blonde to Light Brown Hair, Medium Skin, Medium Eyes

W_____ – Red/Auburn/Golden Hair, Skin & Eyes Vary

## Star Power: Embrace Your Frame

5'2" & under  _____  Girl
5'3" to 5'7"  _____  Star
5'8" & taller  _____  Star

## Shape Up Your Style – Dress With Grace & Confidence

**B - Fuller Belly Tips:**

Flowy fabrics; avoid tight waistlines

V-neck tops flatter the face and lengthen the look

Sleeve hems should NOT stop at the waist

"Column Dressing" = similar color top and bottom, contrast jacket

**O - Fuller Bust/Midriff Tips:**

Wrap or empire waist dresses

V-neck without cleavage; short necklaces

Heels elongate – you've got great legs

Printed tops and 3/4 sleeves work well

Inside Column – colors match or blend – different color for layering gives balance

**D - Fuller Hips & Thighs Tips:**

Tops should end above or below widest point

Add width up top with scarves, pads, or wide necklines

Flare or straight-leg pants

Belts are your friend

Outside Column – Jacket and pants should match/blend

### X - Balanced or All-Over Weight Gain:

You are already proportioned—wear most styles confidently

Address secondary areas if needed

## Who's Got Style? YOU Do!

Style Personalities:

_____ **Chic** – Loves cotton, silk, linen, sophisticated ease

_____ **Original** – Artistic combinations, bold patterns

_____ **Modern** – Timeless elegance, pearls, tailored pieces

**Style** _____ – Trend-loving, bold accessorizing, runway flair

## 'PRAISE ON WEAR' - Your POW Outfit!

Makes you say WOW

Feels great and looks amazing

Reflects "your" personality and values

### Look for:

A trending color

- Eye-catching pattern or details
- Soft, quality fabric (e.g., satin, charmeuse)
- Unique style – shape

**The Vital V – First Impressions Count!**

This "V" area from your shoulders down is where the eye lands first.

Keep necklines and accessory lengths proportionate to your face and neck.

- Long neck? Chokers (15–17")
- Short neck? Longer necklaces (18–20")
- Matching your "Vital V" skin space with your facial features creates visual harmony.

## What to Wear & When

### Networking / Meet & Greet

- Dress professionally – add your personal touch
- Carry business cards
- When in doubt, dress up slightly

### Breakout Speaker

- Dress one level above the audience
- Add color to be engaging and visible
- Style should match your message and personality

## Day 3

**Large Stage**

    Dress for visibility from the back row

    Avoid black if standing against a black background

    Skip small prints/tiny stripes that "dance" on camera

    Go bold with lip color and clean, noise-free jewelry

    Wear stylish shoes that don't hurt

    Clothing with movement adds flair on stage

## Final Tip from Judy:

*You are God's masterpiece—reflect that beauty with joy, boldness, and grace!*

_____

_____

_____

_____

_____

_____

_____

_____

_____

# Saturday

# Daily Reflection

### Joshua 1:9 (NIV)

*"Have I not commanded you? Be strong and courageous. Do not be afraid; do not be discouraged, for the Lord your God will be with you wherever you go."*

Today is not just another day. It's a step into the **calling** God has prepared for you. He's not only planned your future—He's walking into it with you. So be strong. Be **courageous**. You don't have to be perfect. You just have to show up. God is with you, and His plans for you are still unfolding.

What is God stirring in your heart regarding your future?

Where is He inviting you to be bold?

# Intro Reel Notes

# Intro Reel Notes

# Sunday

## Daily Reflection

Matthew 9:36–38 (NIV)

*When he saw the crowds, he had compassion on them, because they were harassed and helpless, like sheep without a shepherd. Then he said to his disciples, "The harvest is plentiful but the workers are few. Ask the Lord of the harvest, therefore, to send out workers into his harvest field."*

The harvest is more than plentiful, and you are part of the answer. You've been called, equipped, and prayed for across generations. It is your time to rise and step into your calling.

Where is God calling you into His harvest field?

What next step will you take in faith?

When the final hug is shared, pause here. Let this be your sacred space to capture what matters most—the truths, the tools, and the tender moments God gave you this weekend.

My three biggest AHA moments:

1. _____

2. _____

3. _____

The most important takeaways that I don't want to forget:

1. _____

2. _____

3. _____

The tools I want to use immediately:

1. _____

2. _____

3. _____

# Day 5

## Commitments to Myself...

This week (when I get home), I will:

Within 30 Days, I will:

Within 90 days, I will:

By the end of this year, I will:

By this time next year (when I return to CCC 2026):

## My Next Brave Step

The one thing I will do differently because of this conference:

How I want to grow in my calling:

My prayer for the journey ahead:

## My Support Network

The women I connected with this weekend:

Mentor

Name: _____

Connect with her at: _____

_____

_____

*Day 5*

Accountability Partner

Name: _____

Connect with her at: _____

_____

_____

Friend

Name: _____

Connect with her at: _____

_____

_____

## Final Thoughts

This was more than a conference—it was a launching pad. You have everything you need to move forward with purpose, boldness, and joy. We are cheering you on in your speaking, your writing, your ministry, and your dreams.

Numbers 6:24-26 (NIV)

*The Lord bless you and keep you; the Lord make his face shine on you and be gracious to you; the Lord turn his face toward you and give you peace.*

Go forth and communicate His love.

# Director

## Pam Mitchael

Pam Mitchael is a speaker and author known for her heartfelt wisdom and Spirit-led storytelling. With warmth, wit, and a few well-placed southern analogies, she shares real-life stories that reflect God's grace—especially in the unexpected detours of life. Her words are both comforting and convicting, spoken from the perspective of a fellow sojourner who knows what it means to trust God through twists and turns.

Pam is passionate about helping women recognize their worth and identity in Christ and empowering them to step boldly into their God-given purpose.

She serves as Director of the Christian Communicators Conference, a speaker training ministry where she blends her 35 years of hospitality leadership with her calling to encourage communicators of faith.

A proud native Texan, Pam lives just down the sidewalk from her three favorite humans—the grandkids who call her "Lolly."

# Speakers

## Linda Goldfarb

Whether sipping frothed coffee with friends, hiking with Sam, engaging in fun activities with her children and grandchildren, or speaking truth with gentle boldness, Linda Goldfarb strives to be transparent and real.

Linda is an award-winning multi-book author and podcaster, a board-certified advanced-level Christian life coach, an audiobook narrator, an international speaker, and a board member of the Advanced Writers and Speakers Association.

She is a frequent keynote speaker, workshop leader, and multi-session continuing class teacher at writer's and speaker's conferences each year. Linda emcees the Blue Ridge Mountains Christian Writers Conference, serving as the third member of The BRMCWC Leadership Team.

Known as the kind of person you are drawn to immediately, Linda is recognized for having a voice that makes you feel welcome, safe, and seen. When she shares her energy, experiences, and expertise during interviews and from the stage, screen, or in her writing, you lean in—not wanting to miss a single word. Linda and her hubby, Sam, are the proud parents of four adult children, numerous grandchildren, and one great-grandson. They live on the edge of the Texas Hill Country with their two rescue pups, MeMe and DJ. Linda credits a combination of faith, humor, and personality awareness with growing their relationship into a thriving adventure lasting more than 38 years.

Linda is quick to share, "My life is far from perfect, and that's where Yeshua met me, loved me, and saved me. For Him, I'm eternally grateful."

## Mary DeMuth

Mary DeMuth is a literary agent, daily podcaster at Pray Every Day Show, Scripture artist, speaker, and the author of 50+ books, including The Most Overlooked Women of the Bible (Skyhorse, 2025). She lives in Texas with her husband and is the mom to three adult children. Find out more at marydemuth.com.

# Speakers

## Mary R. Snyder

Mary Snyder is the speaker whisperer, storytelling coach, and go-to expert for Christian speakers and events. With over two decades of experience, she's mastered both sides of the stage—captivating audiences with her own dynamic presence and coaching some of today's most influential speakers to craft compelling messages that hit the mark.

Mary's unique blend of speaker expertise and storytelling strategy makes her the ultimate guide for anyone looking to elevate their speaking game. Whether you're fine-tuning your message or preparing for a major event, Mary's got you covered with her signature style and proven techniques. And if you want a taste of her insights, tune in to the StorySpire Podcast, where she shares practical tips and storytelling wisdom with a sassy twist.

## Andrea Lende

Andrea Lende is the go-to guide for faith-filled speakers who want to turn their God-given messages into published works. As a bestselling and award-winning author, speaker, and CEO of Beatitudes Publishing, Andrea doesn't just help women publish books, she helps them share their stories with clarity, courage, and Kingdom purpose.

Whether she's helping craft devotionals, hosting award-winning anthologies like *Strength in the Storm*, or teaching practical self-publishing strategies, Andrea brings a rare blend of compassion and know-how to every woman and her project. Andrea's workshops and live sessions are packed with step-by-step wisdom, and her savvy messaging helps Christian authors get seen, get downloaded, and get known—without losing their voice or values.

If you're a speaker who's ever whispered, "Is this story really worth writing about?" Andrea's already cheering you on. She knows your words matter, and she's here to help you share them with the world.

# Speakers

## Victoria Chapin

Victoria Chapin is a speaker and author who inspires others to embrace adversity and live abundantly in Christ.

Her passion to "do life to the full", despite tragedy, encourages women towards intimacy with God and to walk boldly in their destiny. Victoria is the Director of The Well Conference for Creatives and serves with her husband Jim as Chaplain and Co-Founder of Do Life 2 The Full Ministries. She has been featured on Christian programming such as FTG Network and barbTV and has been a guest on multiple podcasts.

Victoria is the author of Undaunted: A Prayer Journal, co-author of the best-selling anthology, Story Matters, and contributing author for the devotional titled, We Get You. She lives in Southwest Michigan and is a mom to many and a Grammy to even more. Victoria loves everything coffee, especially when shared with friends.

Sign up for my monthly newsletter for freebies, tips, and what's trending!
Visit me at victoriachapin.com to subscribe and receive special offers just for my CCC sisters!

## Kim Kimble

A resident of Johnson County, Texas since 1970 and a Burleson High School graduate from the class of 1979, Kim Kimble wears multiple hats as a wife, mom, Grammy, and business owner. Prior to selling houses she worked as a Catering Manager and event planner in the hospitality industry.

It wasn't until she followed her heart to begin Hope Encounter Women's Conference that she realized her experience in that industry merely prepared her for God's calling to plan a once a year event that would bring Hope and unity to women in her local area.

Kim currently resides in Joshua with her husband of 35 years. They are proud parents of two children, Shane and Lindsay, grandparents to Moriah, Noah, Charlie, and Ember, and great-grandparents to Lailah.

# Speakers

## Judy Bone

Judy Bone, author of IN HIS GLOW: Guiding You to God's Bright and Beautiful Path, infuses her unique Southern charm and humor into her inspiring story of triumph over esophageal cancer. In her book, Judy shares her journey of navigating illness with unwavering faith and infectious optimism, uplifting everyone who reads her personal story.

As a Christian Image Consultant, Judy empowers women to discover their best fashion choices, helping them select colors, styles, and accessories that enhance their God-given beauty.

Her guidance extends beyond aesthetics; she provides practical tools and spiritual insights to cultivate confidence in women of all ages and body shapes.

Get ready to be inspired by Judy! Drawing from her rich experiences as a minister's wife, she truly understands women's unique challenges. Her "Let's Get Glowing" message is a heartfelt invitation for you to embrace the joy of living a life illuminated by Jesus' light.

Whether you're part of a large crowd or an intimate gathering, Judy's vibrant presence will uplift you, reminding you that life is about more than just existing. It's about celebrating laughter-filled moments and experiencing God's grace in your journey. You won't want to miss this opportunity to shine brighter together!

## Angela Driskell

Angela Driskell has over 20 years of experience in branding, graphic design, and website development. As the founder of Journey Websites, Angela and her global team partner with Christian writers, speakers, and small business owners to help them share their unique stories. Angela's professional background includes work as a Firefighter, Public Education Officer, and Senior Advisor at Apple. Her passion for empowering others shines through her ability to translate "tech speak" into easy-to-understand language.

Angela lives in Indiana with her husband Bryan, two fur-babies, and she can be found on the field shooting sports photography during Notre Dame football games!

# Praise and Worship

## Lauren Lindsey

Lauren Lindsey has dedicated over 21 years to pastoral ministry, passionately guiding others in their walk with Christ. Alongside her husband, she answered God's call to plant Brave Church in Missouri City three years ago, creating a vibrant community centered on worship, discipleship, and service. As a devoted mother to three daughters—ages 19, 15, and 7—Lauren's life is a testament to God's faithfulness across generations.

For over two decades, Lauren has faithfully led worship, pouring her heart into creating spaces where people can "enter his gates with thanksgiving" and "go into his courts with praise" (Psalm 100:4, NLT). She believes deeply in the power of worship to usher people into God's presence, where they can experience His grace and love in transformative ways.

Guided by Jesus' words in Matthew 5:14-16, "You are the light of the world—like a city on a hilltop that cannot be hidden...let your good deeds shine out for all to see, so that everyone will praise your heavenly Father" (NLT), Lauren is committed to reflecting Christ's light in everything she does. She also seeks to use the anointing on her life to help women break free from chains that hold them bound, empowering them to walk in the freedom and fullness God has for them.

# Sponsors

**MARY R.** *Snyder*

Mary R. Snyder
The Power of Storytelling
Visit Mary's website for an overview of her business and services:
MaryRSnyder.com

**Beach Retreat 2026 isn't just a getaway—it's a pause with a purpose.**

March 3–6 | Gulf Shores, Alabama

This retreat is for women who've walked the road of speaking, who know God is calling them to speak, and who know what it means to carry a meaningful message.

You've been pouring out—and now it's time to pause, breathe, and let God pour back into you.

Picture this: mornings by the water, Spirit-led worship, deep conversations with women who get it, and the kind of laughter that makes your stomach hurt in the best way. Add a splash of bold teaching, a dash of beachy fun, and more than a few moments of **Surprise & Delight.**

This retreat isn't about hustle. It's about holy reset—realigning your heart with what matters most and remembering the calling that set this whole thing in motion.

Spots are limited, and we're already halfway full. The retreat sold out last year. This is your last chance to grab the 10-month payment plan.

If your soul whispered "yes" while reading this…
Scan the QR code.
Your beach chair (and your breakthrough) is waiting.

Let's do this together.

# Sponsors

**Beatitudes Publishing**
Helping Christian Authors Publish with Purpose

Beatitudes Publishing is a premier self-publishing company devoted to helping Christian speakers and writers transform their God-given messages into professionally published books.

Beatitudes Publishing offers a full suite of personalized services, including:

- Book coaching and publishing strategy
- Developmental and copy editing
- Manuscript formatting and custom cover design
- Audiobook production
- Amazon optimization and metadata support

From blank page to bookstore shelves, we'll help you share your story with clarity, confidence, and Kingdom impact. Visit us at beatitudespublishing.com to learn more.

We're gathering stories for an anthology, *Successful in His Eyes*, and we'd love to include yours. If you've experienced a moment when God redefined success for you—through surrender, faith, or simply showing up—we invite you to share it. CCC attendees are welcome to submit a brief one- to two-paragraph summary for possible inclusion.

Last year, *Strength in the Storm* was an Amazon bestseller and received the Silver Selah Award. We invite you to join the Beatitudes writers. Let's change the world with our words!

Email your submission to andrea@andrealende.com by July 31.

*Sponsors*

# Judy Bone
### Let's Get Glowing!

## Judy Bone
### Speaker — Author — Image Consultant

Judy Bone is a dynamic speaker with a heart for encouraging women to shine with confidence, inside and out. A survivor of esophageal cancer and author of In His Glow, Judy weaves her testimony with biblical truth to help women walk in resilience, purpose, and radiant faith. As a Certified Christian Image Consultant, she also equips women in ministry to present themselves with Goauthenticity and grace, reflecting the beauty of Christ in every setting. Whether through keynote messages or breakout sessions, Judy brings warmth, wisdom, and practical insight to help women GLOW for God in their unique callings. Please reach out to Judy to explore how she can help your audience find hope, identity, and purpose.

**Contact: flocklady@gmail.com**

*"He makes all things beautiful in His time."*
Ecclesiastes 3:11

## Sponsors

### CCC Special 20% off all Coaching Bundles
Offer Ends 7/31/2025
LGoldfarb5@gmail.com Subject: CCC Coaching Special

**Linda Goldfarb**
Keynote & Retreat Speaker
Relationship Thought Leader
Certified Christian Life Coach
Award-winning Podcaster
Award-winning Author

Your Next Best Step Awaits…
is it time for a change?

Grow Personally & Professionally

Move from Stuck to Standing Out

Discover Your Podcasting & Audiobook Options

LinkedPersonalityQuiz.com
Linda@LindaGoldfarb.com

www.LindaGoldfarb.com
facebook.com/linda.goldfarb
Your Best Writing Life Podcast
Staying Real About Faith & Family Podcast

**Journey Websites**
with Angela Driskell

JourneyWebsites.com
Hello@JourneyWebsites.com

Helping you share your story…

## Sponsors

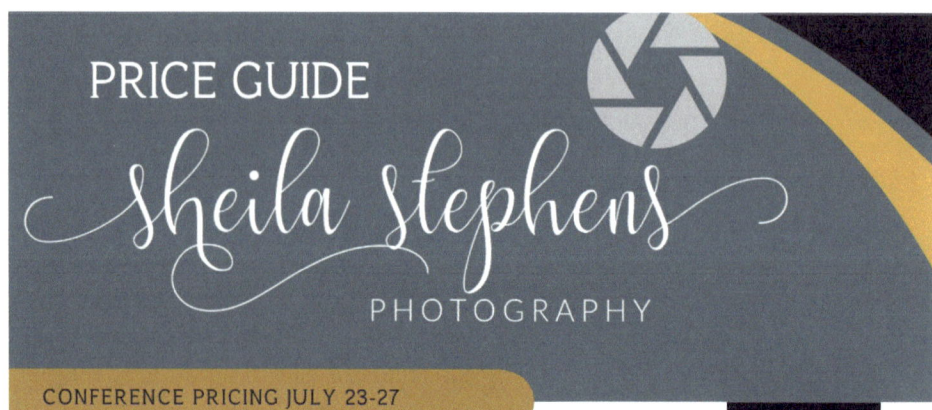

### PRICE GUIDE
### sheila stephens
#### PHOTOGRAPHY

**CONFERENCE PRICING JULY 23-27**

$199

- All Professionally Edited Images Included
- Personalized Branding Session*
- High-resolution digital images
- Online gallery for viewing

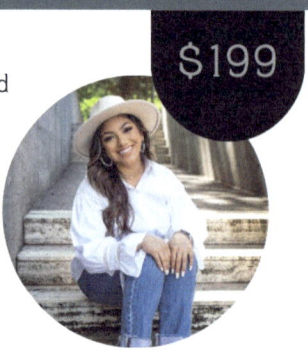

**POST CONFERENCE AFTER JULY 27**

$500

- All Professionally Edited Images Included
- Personalized Branding Session*
- High-resolution digital images
- Online gallery for viewing

**INDIVIDUAL DIGITAL IMAGE PRICING**

**Conference Pricing July 23-27:**
$20 Per Image

**Post Conference Pricing:**
$45 Per Image

*ALL ATTENDEES WILL RECEIVE 1 FREE IMAGE WITH THEIR COMPLIMENTARY MINI HEADSHOT/BRANDING SESSION

# Sponsors

## Tracey Glenn
### SIZZLE REEL VIDEO PACKAGES
Website: traceyglenn.com
emali: tglenn@brandedinfaith.com

**A** — *Complimentary Raw Footage* — No Charge!

**B** — Conference Special $200 — **Basic Package** — Regular Price $250

Included: Intro with Message Title & Speaker Name / Music / Logo (Optional-Speaker Provides) / One Brand Colors (Speaker provides hex code) / One Still Image Add-In (Speaker provides) / Outro Slide with Contact Information /

View Examples

**C** — Conference Special $499 — **Pro-Package** — Regular Price $600

Includes Package B Elements Plus: Provide up to 1 extra video of you speaking, and I will pull out dynamic portions from that video to create a seamless message. Tag Line or Ministry Name on Animated Intro / One Additional Brand Color (2 Colors Total) / Into-Outro Video (Speaker will provide video) / Up to 5 Still Images (Speaker provides) / Up to 2 Word-Over Bible verses, or Quotes (Speaker provides) / Website address appearing throughout video.

View Example

**D** — Conference Special $599 — **ProPlus-Package** — Regular $800

Includes Package B & C Elements Plus: Provide up to 3 videos of you speaking, and I will pull out dynamic portions from each to create a seamless message. Other extras include: Up to 5 video or written testimonials (Speaker provides). Your Website plus Book Now scrolled throughout the video. Dynamic Display of 10-15 Still Images (Speaker Provides Images).
Don't have 10-15 still images? No Worries! I will create up to 5 for you.

View Examples

## CCC Workbook
## designed by

## Beatitudes Publishing

beatitudespublishing.com

A special thank you to Tracey Glenn, whose creativity and dedication brought the vision for this book to life.

Made in the USA
Columbia, SC
15 July 2025